Table of Contents

Executive Summary

This report summarizes non-fire carbon monoxide (CO) incidents associated with engine-driven generators and other engine-driven tools that occurred between 1999 and 2011, and were reported to the U.S. Consumer Product Safety Commission (CPSC) staff as of April 20, 2012. It should be noted that due to incident reporting delays, statistics for the most recent years should be considered incomplete. In this report, the two most recent years, 2010 and 2011, are identified as being incomplete since these figures are most likely to change in future reports. Throughout this report, the number of deaths represents a count of the fatalities reported to CPSC staff associated with generators and other engine-driven tools, such as power lawn mowers, garden tractors, portable pumps, power sprayers and washers, snow blowers, and concrete saws. Also included in this report are summaries of fatal, non-fire CO incidents, where an engine-driven tool (EDT) and one or more other fuel-burning consumer products[1] also may have been involved and the EDT was believed to be, at least, a contributing factor to the fatal levels of CO. These fatalities are characterized in the "Multiple Product" category. This report also provides a more detailed summary of fatal, non-fire CO poisoning incidents associated with engine-driven tools, with particular emphasis on cases involving generator use, based on information found in the CPSC's In-depth Investigation (INDP) File.

Some of the findings of this report are provided below.

CO Fatalities Associated with All EDTs and by EDT Product Type:

- The total number of fatalities for 1999 through 2011 increased by 141 from the 740 fatalities summarized in the July 2011 report, which reported fatalities for the period 1999 through 2010 as of February 17, 2011. Fifty-three of the newly recorded fatalities occurred prior to 2011. This is a larger than usual number and can be attributed to a later-than-usual cut-off date for reports than the prior year (April instead of February) and a larger-than-usual number of late death certificate submissions from a few states.

- From 1999 through 2011, 881 fatalities from 680 fatal incidents were associated with the use of engine-driven tools, or engine-driven tools used in conjunction with another potentially CO-emitting consumer product.

- As of April 20, 2012, there were 88 reported non-fire CO fatalities in 2011, from 62 incidents. Seventy-three of these deaths (49 incidents) involved only a generator and no other product; 8 deaths (8 incidents) were associated with a non-generator other engine-driven tool (OEDT); and 7 deaths (5 incidents) were associated with multiple fuel-burning consumer products, one of which was a generator.

- From 1999 to 2011, 695 (79%) of the 881 fatalities from 513 incidents were associated with generators; 121 fatalities (14%) from 118 incidents involved other engine-driven tools; and 65 fatalities (7%) from 49 incidents involved multiple fuel-burning consumer products, one product of which was a generator (59 of 65 deaths) or OEDT (5 of 65 deaths) or both a generator and an OEDT (1 of 65 deaths).

---

[1] Combustion consumer products produce heat or energy by burning a fuel source. It should be noted that all fuel-burning consumer products may produce gases that contain CO because CO is a by-product of incomplete combustion.

- Of the 49 incidents that involved multiple consumer products, all but two incidents involved a heating or cooking product, most commonly a portable LP- or kerosene-fueled portable heater. One incident involved a generator and an OEDT (a lawnmower), and another incident involved two gasoline-fueled OEDTs (a lawnmower and trimmer).
- Twenty-six percent of generator-related, non-fire CO incidents caused multiple fatalities, while only three of the OEDT-related incidents (3%) involved multiple fatalities. Twenty-seven percent of multiple product-related, non-fire CO incidents caused multiple fatalities.
- Nearly three-fourths (553 of 755) of generator-related fatalities detailed in this report (including fatalities involving multiple products where one product was a generator) occurred between 2005 and 2011.

Socio-Demographic Characteristics of Victims and EDT-Use Patterns:
- Eighty-three percent of generator-related victims (including multiple product incidents where a generator was involved) were known to be 25 years old or older, where the age of the victims was known. By contrast, 99 percent of OEDT-related victims were 25 years old or older.
- Nearly three-quarters of the generator-related, non-fire CO victims were male, while 97 percent (all but four) of the OEDT-related fatalities were male.
- Nearly half (49%), of generator-related, non-fire CO fatalities (371 of 755, including multiple product incidents) occurred in the four colder months of the year (November through February), while CO fatalities associated with OEDTs were only slightly more prevalent in the colder months (40%) than in the transitional and warm months (34% and 25%, respectively).
- Seventy-three percent of the generator-related fatalities and 75 percent of fatalities from multiple products, where one was a generator, occurred in fixed-structure homes, while 59 percent of OEDT fatalities occurred in fixed-structure homes.
- Fifty-five percent of the EDT-related fatalities are known to have occurred in urban areas. Seventeen percent occurred in small rural and isolated areas, nearly double the proportion of the U.S. population that lives in such areas.

CO Alarm Usage:
- A CO alarm was reported to have been present in only 21 of 265 incidents where alarm presence was known, which accounted for 30 of 368 (8%) EDT-related CO fatalities. In nine of the incidents (16 deaths), the alarm was inoperable due to no batteries, batteries inserted incorrectly, or no electric current. The alarm sounded in six incidents (six deaths), and in three incidents (three deaths), the alarm was powered but did not sound. Additionally, there were three incidents (five deaths) in which the presence of a CO alarm was noted, but it is unknown if the alarm sounded during the event.

Hazard Patterns Associated with Generators:
- Twenty-nine percent of all generator-related, non-fire CO deaths (220 of 755) were associated with power outages. Of these 220 fatalities, 53 (24%) occurred in 2005. Thirty-one of the 2005 fatalities were related to hurricanes or tropical storms, and another 20 were related to ice or snow storms. (Additionally, one fatality was associated with a

thunderstorm; and for one fatality, it could not be determined what caused the power outage.)

- Five hundred and fifty-one non-fire CO fatalities that occurred in fixed-structure homes were associated with a generator or a generator in use with another CO-generating consumer product. Seventy percent (385 of 551) occurred when the generator was placed inside the living area of the home, including the basement, closets, and doorways, but excluding the attached garage, enclosed carport, or attached barn.
- In recent years, the most common location of generators associated with CO fatalities has shifted from the basement to the non-basement living space of the home. From 2004 through 2011, 38 percent (169 of 442) of CO fatalities in the home occurred with a generator placed in the non-basement living space of the home, compared to only 21 percent (23 of 109) of non-basement use of generators from 1999 through 2003.
- Nearly two-thirds (66%; 205 of 312) of generator-related, non-fire CO fatalities in fixed-structure homes (for which information on ventilation of the generator was available) occurred when no ventilation of the generator was attempted.
- Sixty-one percent (215 of 353) of generator-related, non-fire CO fatalities in fixed-structure homes, where the size of the home was known and the generator was not located in an external structure, occurred in houses less than 1,500 square feet in size; 84 percent (298 of 353) occurred in houses less than 2,000 square feet in size.
- Two-thirds (67%; 245 of 367) of CO fatalities where the size of the generator was known were associated with generators in the 3500 to 6499 watt range, and nearly half (46%; 168 of 367) were associated with generators in the 5000 to 6499 watt range.

Carboxyhemoglobin Levels in CO Fatality Victims:
- Of the CO fatality victims associated with engine-driven tools, more than 81 percent had carboxyhemoglobin (COHb) levels above the 50 percent level when the COHb level was known (405 of 499).[2]

Note: Throughout this report, the years 2010 and 2011 are italicized in table headings, indicating that incident and death counts may change as additional information is received. Incident and death counts may change for other years but to a much smaller extent.

---

[2] As levels rise above 40 percent COHb, death is possible in healthy individuals and becomes increasingly likely with prolonged exposures that maintain levels in the 40 percent to 60 percent range.

Introduction

The following U.S. Consumer Product Safety Commission (CPSC) databases were searched to prepare the statistics recorded in this report: the In-depth Investigation (INDP) File, the Injury or Potential Injury Incident (IPII) File, and the Death Certificate (DTHS) File. See Appendix A for the codes and keywords used in the database searches. The data records were combined and collated to develop the most complete records possible in a single database. At this stage, each record was reviewed to determine if the incident was in scope for this report and to correct any discrepancies between information from the different sources. (See Appendix A for the specifics of scope determination.) It should be noted that reporting may not be complete, and this report reflects only those incidents reported and entered into CPSC databases on or before April 20, 2012. All fatal, unintentional, non-fire carbon monoxide (CO) incidents associated with engine-driven tools (EDTs) found during the database search that were determined to be in scope were included.

CPSC records contain information on 881 non-fire CO fatalities associated with EDTs during the years 1999 through 2011. This is an increase of 141 fatalities from the 740 fatalities reported in the July 2011 report on non-fire CO fatalities associated with EDTs which included data entered in CPSC databases as of February 17, 2011.[3] Eighty-eight of these 141 fatalities occurred in 2011, while the remaining 53 occurred in previous years but were reported after the July 2011 report. Eighty-one of the 88 fatalities were associated with generators or other engine-driven tools (OEDT) as the only known source of the CO. Seven additional fatalities were associated with multiple, combustion fuel-burning consumer products. Incidents associated with generators that were specifically reported as integral parts of recreational vehicles (RVs), motor homes, or boats are not within the jurisdiction of the CPSC, and thus, were considered out of scope and were not included. For example, generators that were reported as mounted to an RV were not included, nor were boat generators that were installed by the boat manufacturer. Since incidents in recreational vehicles and boats can be associated with a portable generator or an integral generator, those incidents in which the type of generator could not be determined were also excluded from the analysis.

Any incident that was determined to be other than accidental in nature was considered to be out of scope, as were work-related incidents, which are not within the jurisdiction of the CPSC.

This report is divided into four sections:

I.   Reported Numbers of Fatalities by EDT Product Type. This presents an overall picture of CO fatalities associated with engine-driven tools.
II. Socio-demographics of Victims and EDT Use Patterns. This presents various socio-demographic summaries helpful in identifying specific characteristics of CO fatality victims and usage patterns, such as when and where fatalities occurred.
III. Alarm Usage. This presents information on CO alarm usage during fatal CO events.

---

[3] Hnatov, M. V. *Incidents, Deaths, and In-Depth Investigations Associated with Non-Fire Carbon Monoxide from Engine-Driven Generators and Other Engine-Driven Tools, 1999–2010. U.S. Consumer Product Safety Commission. July 2011.*

IV.   Hazard Patterns Associated with Generators. This presents data specific to generator usage patterns that may lead to fatal CO poisoning events.

Additionally, Appendix B presents summary findings on carboxyhemoglobin levels in the blood of victims of CO poisoning involving EDT use, which are helpful in assessing the hazard presented by the product and the speed of onset of harm.

I. Reported Numbers of Fatalities by Engine-Driven Tool (EDT) Product Type

As of April 20, 2012, CPSC staff had records indicating that there were 62 fatal, non-fire carbon monoxide (CO) exposure incidents involving engine-driven tools between January 1, 2011 and December 31, 2011. Eighty-eight deaths occurred in these 62 fatal CO incidents. Table 1 presents the reported fatal incidents and the number of deaths in 2011, along with a summary of CO incidents and fatalities associated with engine-driven tools for the 13-year period from 1999 through 2011. The table records the number of incidents and deaths by the broad categories of "Generators," "Other Engine-Driven Tools," and "Multiple Products." Multiple product incidents are fatal CO poisonings that involved multiple fuel-burning consumer products that generate CO, at least one being an EDT, or in which investigating authorities could not determine which of multiple consumer products in use at the time of the incident was the source of the CO. CPSC staff is aware of 65 fatalities associated with multiple consumer products occurring between 1999 and 2011; seven of these fatalities occurred in 2011. Multiple product incidents where one of the sources of CO is not under the CPSC's jurisdiction, such as automobiles, boats, or recreational vehicles, were determined to be out of scope and are not included in this report.

It should be noted that fatality and incident counts from years prior to 2011 may have changed from the previous report. The changes are due primarily to the addition of new data that were made available to CPSC staff. New to this report are 53 reported fatalities that occurred before 2011, and 88 fatalities that occurred in 2011.

Within each broad category, the frequency of reports is summarized by product type. Staff is aware of 680 incidents with a total of 881 deaths due to non-fire CO exposure that occurred between 1999 and 2011, involving engine-driven tools.

In Table 1, the product type "welder" appears in both the "Generator" and "Other Engine-Driven Tool" categories. Some welding equipment is designed to be used as a welder or as an electric generator. Two of the fatal, non-fire CO incidents associated with the use of welding equipment that occurred between 1999 and 2011, involved the use of the welder as a generator during a power outage. Each of these two incidents involved a single death. There were six fatal, non-fire CO incidents between 1999 and 2011 that were associated with the use of welder equipment, where it was not specifically identified as being used as a generator. Of these six incidents, one incident (involving two deaths) occurred when the welder was being used as a source of heat, and, in the other five incidents (six deaths: four single-fatality incidents and one two-fatality incident), the welder was being used for welding purposes or the method of usage could not be ascertained. These latter five incidents were included in the "Other Engine-Driven Tools" category because there was no evidence indicating that the welders were being used as generators.

In 2011, there were three incidents (five fatalities) involving non-portable, fixed-location generators that were either installed inside the home or were located too close to a vent or window, allowing CO to enter the home. This category has been added to Table 1. However, these incidents will be included in the "Generator" category for further analysis similar to the scenarios involving welders used as generators.

All but two of the 65 non-fire, CO fatalities in the "Multiple Products" category for 1999–2011 involved a heating- or cooking-related consumer product other than an EDT. One incident involved a generator and a lawn tractor being run in a closed garage. The other incident involved a gasoline-fueled walk behind mower and gasoline-fueled trimmer also running in a closed garage.

Table 1: Number of Reported Fatal Non-Fire Carbon Monoxide Exposure Incidents and Deaths Associated with Engine-Driven Tools, 1999–*2011*

Product	*2011*		Total: 1999–*2011*	
	Number of Incidents	*Number of Deaths*	Number of Incidents	Number of Deaths
Total Engine-Driven Tools	*62*	*88*	680	881
Generators	*49*	*73*	513	695
Generator, portable	*46*	*68*	508	688
Generator, fixed	*3*	*5*	3	5
Welder (used as a generator)[1]	*0*	*0*	2	2
Other Engine-Driven Tools (OEDT)	*8*	*8*	118	121
Riding lawn mower/Garden tractor	*5*	*5*	62	62
Push lawn mower	*0*	*0*	3	3
Powered lawn mower, unspecified type	*0*	*0*	5	5
Power washer/sprayer	*1*	*1*	9	9
Snow blower	*1*	*1*	11	11
All-terrain vehicle	*0*	*0*	7	8
Welder (used as welder or other reason)[1]	*0*	*0*	6	8
Water pump	*0*	*0*	4	4
Concrete saw	*0*	*0*	3	3
Air compressor	*0*	*0*	2	2
Paint sprayer	*0*	*0*	1	1
Snowmobile	*0*	*0*	1	1
Go-cart	*0*	*0*	1	1
Tiller	*0*	*0*	1	1
Small engine (unknown use)	*0*	*0*	1	1
Edger	*1*	*1*	1	1
Multiple Products[2]	*5*	*7*	49	65
Generator + Other Consumer Product[3]	*5*	*7*	44	60
OEDT + Other Consumer Product	*0*	*0*	5	5

1   Some welding equipment is designed to be used as either a welder or a generator.
2   "Multiple Products" includes incidents involving generators or OEDTs with other combustion fuel-burning consumer products. "Other Consumer Products" includes one or more of the following: portable LP-fueled heaters, portable kerosene-fueled heaters, camp stoves, lanterns, outdoor cookers, furnaces, and wood stoves, and one case with a generator and an OEDT (lawn tractor) in operation.
3   This category includes one incident involving one fatality where a generator and an OEDT were being used concurrently.
Note: Italicized numbers indicate that reporting of incidents is ongoing. Counts may change in subsequent reports.
Source: U. S. Consumer Product Safety Commission, Directorate for Epidemiology, 2012.

Five hundred-thirteen of the 680 incidents reported to CPSC staff were associated with a generator and accounted for 695 of the 881 CO deaths (79%). Additionally, 60 other CO fatalities from 44 incidents were associated with the use of a generator and another combustion consumer product—most commonly an LP- or kerosene-fueled heater. One of these fatalities involved a generator and another engine-driven tool (lawn tractor). For the rest of this report, this incident will be included in the tables and discussions in the category *Multiple Products* involving a generator. Throughout the remainder of this report, incidents associated with all non-generator engine-driven tools are reported as a group. In addition, because the majority of incidents were associated with generators, characteristics of these incidents are reported separately in Section IV. More than half of the non-fire, non-generator CO fatalities (62 of 121) involved a garden tractor or other powered lawn mower (including multiple product incidents). Deaths associated with powered lawn mowers were often associated with an individual repairing or working on the product in an enclosed space.

CPSC staff examined the number of deaths associated with each fatal incident (Table 2). Of the 680 fatal incidents, 78 percent involved a single fatality. Seventy-four percent (379 of 513) of the fatal generator-related incidents involved a single fatality. One incident involving a generator resulted in the deaths of six individuals, and two others involved five fatalities, one of these five-fatality incidents occurred in 2011. Of the 118 fatal incidents in the "Other Engine-Driven Tools" category, three incidents resulted in more than one fatality. Twenty-six percent of multiple-product, fatal CO incidents resulted in multiple fatalities.

Table 2: Number of Reported Fatal Non-Fire Carbon Monoxide Exposure Incidents and Deaths Associated with Engine-Driven Tools by Number of Deaths per Incident, 1999–*2011*

Number of Deaths Reported in Incident[1]	Total		Generator		Other Engine-Driven Tools		Multiple Products[2,3]	
All Incidents	680	100%	513	100%	118	100%	49 (44)	100%
1	530	78%	379	74%	115	97%	36 (31)	73%
2	113	17%	100	19%	3	3%	10 (10)	20%
3	26	4%	23	4%	0	0%	3 (3)	6%
4	8	1%	8	2%	0	0%	0 (0)	0%
5	2	< 1%	2	< 1%	0	0%	0 (0)	0%
6	1	< 1%	1	< 1%	0	0%	0 (0)	0%

1   SPECIAL NOTE ABOUT COUNTS IN THIS TABLE ONLY: One incident included in this table involved an in-scope, generator-related death and an out-of-scope death (work related). Because two fatalities were involved in the incident, this incident is included as a two-fatality incident. The out-of-scope fatality is not included elsewhere in the report. Therefore, in this table only, there is one additional fatality reported. The fatality was a generator-related fatality, so it is included in the "Generator" and "Total" columns.

2   "Multiple Products" includes incidents involving generators or OEDTs with other combustion fuel-burning consumer products. "Other Consumer Products" includes one or more of the following: portable LP-fueled heaters, portable kerosene-fueled heaters, camp stoves, lanterns, outdoor cookers, furnaces, and wood stoves, and one case with a generator and another engine-driven tool (lawn tractor) in operation.

3   Numbers in parentheses indicate incidents involving a generator and another product, including a case where a generator and an OEDT (lawn mower) were used concurrently.

Notes: Totals may not add to 100 percent due to rounding.
        Italicized numbers indicate that reporting of incidents is ongoing. Counts may change in subsequent reports.
Source: U. S. Consumer Product Safety Commission, Directorate for Epidemiology, 2012.

CPSC staff summarized the number of reported deaths associated with engine-driven tools by year of death (Table 3). It should be noted that the values in Table 3 represent the number of deaths reported to CPSC staff as of April 20, 2012. Some deaths are reported to CPSC staff shortly after an incident occurs, while other deaths are reported to CPSC staff months or even years after an incident occurs. Therefore, counts for more recent years may not be as complete as counts for earlier years and may change in the future. Fifty-three of the 141 reported fatalities new to the report were for years prior to 2011. For the 13 years covered by this report, 71 percent (629 of 881) of the deaths were reported in the most recent seven years (2005 through 2011).

The average number of non-fire CO fatalities associated with both generators and other engine-driven tools for years 2007 through 2009 is also presented in Table 3. These three years represent the most recent years for which CPSC staff believe reporting is substantially complete. Due to reporting delays, these averages may change slightly in the future when data are complete. Figure 1 illustrates the trend in generator-related, non-fire CO fatalities since 1999.

Table 3: Number of Reported Fatal Non-Fire Carbon Monoxide Exposure Incidents and Deaths Associated with Engine-Driven Tools by Year, 1999–2011

Year	Total		Generators		Other Engine-Driven Tools		Multiple Products[1,2]	
	Incidents	Deaths	Incidents	Deaths	Incidents	Deaths	Incidents	Deaths
Total	*680*	*881*	*513*	*695*	*118*	*121*	*49 (44)*	*65 (60)*
1999	12	12	6	6	5	5	1 (0)	1 (0)
2000	22	28	14	20	7	7	1 (1)	1 (1)
2001	19	25	14	17	2	2	3 (3)	6 (6)
2002	47	58	34	42	8	9	5 (4)	7 (6)
2003	51	67	38	52	9	9	4 (3)	6 (5)
2004	50	62	34	46	14	14	2 (1)	2 (1)
2005	93	116	73	94	13	13	7 (7)	9 (9)
2006	80	111	60	89	16	16	4 (4)	6 (6)
2007	68	81	53	65	11	11	4 (4)	5 (5)
2008	76	101	63	87	6	6	7 (6)	8 (7)
2009	56	77	44	65	10	10	2 (2)	2 (2)
2010	*44*	*55*	*31*	*39*	*9*	*11*	*4 (4)*	*5 (5)*
2011	*62*	*88*	*49*	*73*	*8*	*8*	*5 (5)*	*7 (7)*
Average: 2007–2009	67	86	53	72	9	9	5 (4)	5 (5)

1   "Multiple Products" includes incidents involving generators or OEDTs with other CO-generating consumer products. "Other Consumer Products" includes one or more of the following: portable LP-fueled heaters, portable kerosene-fueled heaters, camp stoves, lanterns, outdoor cookers, furnaces, and wood stoves, and one case with a generator and another engine-driven tool (lawn tractor) in operation.

2   Numbers in parentheses indicate incidents involving a generator and another product, including the case where a generator and an OEDT (lawn tractor) were used concurrently.

Notes: Detail averages may not sum to total average due to rounding.
      Italicized numbers indicate that reporting of incidents is ongoing. Counts may change in subsequent reports.

Source: U. S. Consumer Product Safety Commission, Directorate for Epidemiology, 2012.

Figure 1: Number of Reported Non-Fire Carbon Monoxide Fatalities Associated with Engine-Driven Tools, 1999–*2011*

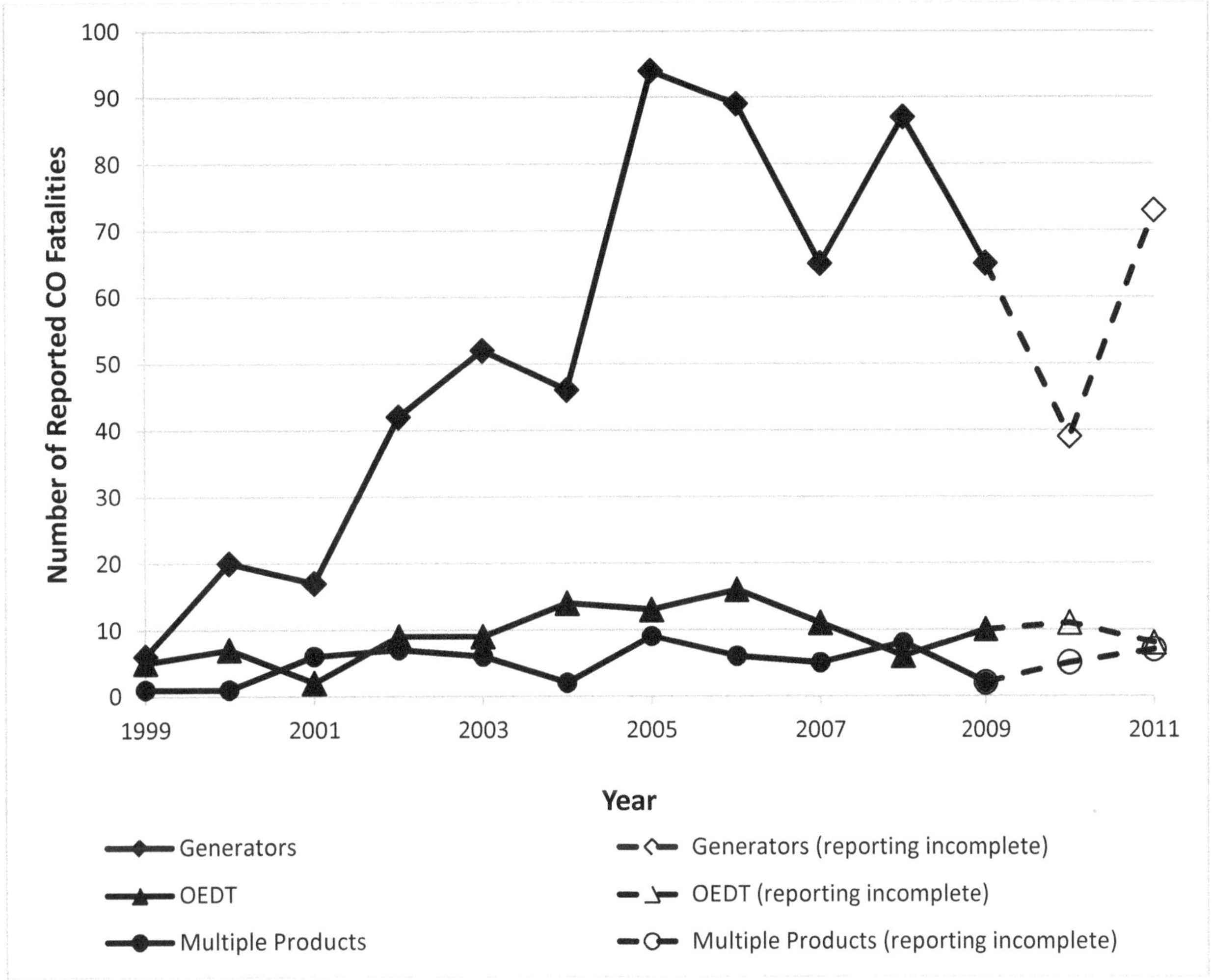

II. Socio-Demographic Characteristics of Victims and EDT Use Patterns

This section presents socio-demographic information about the victims of reported fatal CO incidents associated with engine-driven tools (EDTs). Tables 4 and 5 present the distribution of age and gender of the victims, respectively. Table 4 shows that victims aged 25 years or older accounted for about 85 percent (745 of 873) of reported non-fire, CO poisoning deaths associated with all engine-driven tools where the victim's age is known. Victims with a reported age of 25 years or older accounted for about 83 percent (620 of 747) of non-fire CO poisoning deaths associated with generators (including multiple product related deaths where one product was a generator) and accounted for nearly all of the deaths associated with other engine-driven tools. Eighty-five percent of the non-fire CO fatalities associated with non-generator engine-driven tools (107 of 126) involved victims age 45 or older, with only one reported fatality of an individual younger than 25. Male victims accounted for 78 percent of the deaths associated with all engine-driven tools when the gender of the victim is known. Male victims comprised 75 percent of the deaths associated with generators and 97 percent of non-generator, engine-driven tool fatalities (Table 5).

Table 4: Number of Reported Non-Fire Carbon Monoxide Fatalities Associated with Engine-Driven Tools by Age of Victim, 1999–*2011*

| Age | Number of Deaths Reported to CPSC | | | | | | | | | | | |
| | All Engine-Driven Tools | | | Generators | | | Other Engine-Driven Tools | | | Multiple Products[1,2] | | |
	Deaths	Percentage of All Cases	Percentage when Age is Known	Deaths	Percentage of All Cases	Percentage when Age is Known	Deaths	Percentage of All Cases	Percentage when Age is Known	Deaths	Percentage of All Cases	Percentage when Age is Known
Total	881	100%	100%	695	100%	100%	121	100%	100%	65 (60)	100%	100%
Under 5	14	2%	2%	14	2%	2%	0	0%	0%	0 (0)	0%	0%
5–14	29	3%	3%	29	4%	4%	0	0%	0%	0 (0)	0%	0%
15–24	85	10%	10%	76	11%	11%	1	1%	1%	8 (8)	12%	12%
25–44	261	30%	30%	226	33%	33%	18	15%	15%	17 (17)	26%	26%
45–64	332	38%	38%	239	34%	35%	62	51%	51%	31 (28)	48%	48%
65 and over	152	17%	17%	103	15%	15%	40	33%	33%	9 (7)	14%	14%
Adult, age unknown	6	1%	-	6	1%	-	0	0%	-	0 (0)	0%	-
Unknown age	2	< 1%	-	2	< 1%	-	0	0%	-	0 (0)	0%	-

1 "Multiple Products" includes incidents involving generators or OEDTs with other CO-generating consumer products. "Other Consumer Products" includes one or more of the following: portable LP-fueled heaters, portable kerosene-fueled heaters, camp stoves, lanterns, outdoor cookers, furnaces, and wood stoves, and one case with a generator and another engine-driven tool (lawn mower) in operation.

2 Numbers in parentheses indicate incidents involving a generator and another product, including the case where a generator and an OEDT (lawn mower) were used concurrently.

Notes: Totals may not add to 100 percent due to rounding.

Italicized numbers indicate that reporting of incidents is ongoing. Counts may change in subsequent reports.

Source: U. S. Consumer Product Safety Commission, Directorate for Epidemiology, 2012.

Table 5: Number of Reported Non-Fire Carbon Monoxide Fatalities Associated with Engine-Driven Tools by Gender of Victim, 1999–*2011*

| Gender | Number of Deaths Reported to CPSC | | | | | | | | | | | |
| | All Engine-Driven Tools | | | Generators | | | All Other Engine-Driven Tools | | | Multiple Products[1,2] | | |
	Deaths	Percentage of All Cases	Percentage when Gender is Known	Deaths	Percentage of All Cases	Percentage when Gender is Known	Deaths	Percentage of All Cases	Percentage when Gender is Known	Deaths	Percentage of All Cases	Percentage when Gender is Known
Total	881	100%	100%	695	100%	100%	121	100%	100%	65 (60)	100%	100%
Male	682	77%	78%	509	73%	74%	117	97%	97%	56 (51)	86%	86%
Female	195	22%	22%	182	26%	26%	4	3%	3%	9 (9)	14%	14%
Unknown	4	< 1%	-	4	1%	-	0	0%	-	0 (0)	0%	-

1   "Multiple Products" includes incidents involving generators or OEDTs with other CO-generating consumer products. "Other Consumer Products" includes one or more of the following: portable LP-fueled heaters, portable kerosene-fueled heaters, camp stoves, lanterns, outdoor cookers, furnaces, and wood stoves, and one case with a generator and another engine-driven tool (lawn mower) in operation.

2   Numbers in parentheses indicate incidents involving a generator and another product, including the case where a generator and an OEDT (lawn mower) were used concurrently.

Notes: Totals may not add to 100 percent due to rounding.
         Italicized numbers indicate that reporting of incidents is ongoing. Counts may change in subsequent reports.

Source: U. S. Consumer Product Safety Commission, Directorate for Epidemiology, 2012.

Staff examined reported deaths associated with engine-driven tools by the time of year that the incident occurred (Table 6). The non-fire CO fatalities were classified into one of three categories, depending on the month in which the incident occurred: Cold months, Warm months, and Transitional months. "Cold months" are defined as November, December, January, and February; "Warm months" as May, June, July, and August; and "Transitional months" as March, April, September, and October.

Nearly half (47%, or 49% when multiple product incidents where a generator was involved) of the non-fire CO deaths associated with generators occurred in the cold months of November through February. Many of the fatalities can be directly associated with the use of generators during power outages due to weather conditions such as ice or snow storms. Thirty-one percent of the generator-related CO deaths occurred in the transitional months of March, April, September, and October. A large portion of the non-fire CO fatalities in the transitional months can be directly associated with the use of generators during power outages due to hurricanes and tropical storms, many of which occurred in September and, to a lesser extent, October. Further details on this issue are presented in Section IV of this report.

For OEDTs, CO fatalities were only slightly more prevalent in the cold months (40%) than the transitional months (34%) and warm months (26%). The *Multiple Products* category had a very large proportion of fatalities in the cold months (75%), with 22 percent in the transitional months and three percent occurring in the warm months. This large percentage of fatalities in the cold months can be explained by examining the other fuel-burning consumer products in use at the time of the deaths. Of the 65 CO fatalities that involved multiple consumer products, 60 involved the use of a generator, and all but two involved a heating or cooking product, most commonly a portable LP- or kerosene-fueled portable heater. Heaters are used almost exclusively in the cold and transitional months.

Table 6: Number of Reported Non-Fire Carbon Monoxide Incidents and Fatalities Associated with Engine-Driven Tools by Season, 1999–*2011*

Season Incident Occurred		Number of Incidents and Deaths Reported to CPSC							
		All Engine-Driven Tools		Generators		Other Engine-Driven Tools		Multiple Products[1,2]	
Total	Incidents	680	100%	513	100%	118	100%	49 (44)	100%
	Deaths	881	100%	695	100%	121	100%	65 (60)	100%
Cold months	Incidents	327	48%	242	47%	48	41%	37 (35)	76%
	Deaths	422	48%	324	47%	49	40%	49 (47)	75%
Transitional months	Incidents	201	30%	152	30%	39	33%	10 (8)	20%
	Deaths	269	31%	214	31%	41	34%	14 (12)	22%
Warm months	Incidents	152	22%	119	23%	31	26%	2 (1)	4%
	Deaths	190	22%	157	23%	31	26%	2 (1)	3%

1   "Multiple Products" includes incidents involving generators or OEDTs with other CO- generating consumer products. "Other Consumer Products" includes one or more of the following: portable LP-fueled heaters, portable kerosene-fueled heaters, camp stoves, lanterns, outdoor cookers, furnaces, and wood stoves, and one case with a generator and another engine-driven tool (lawn mower) in operation.

2   Numbers in parentheses indicate incidents involving a generator and another product, including the case where a generator and an OEDT (lawn mower) were being used concurrently.

Notes: Totals may not add to 100 percent due to rounding.

      Italicized numbers indicate that reporting of incidents is ongoing. Counts may change in subsequent reports.

Source: U. S. Consumer Product Safety Commission, Directorate for Epidemiology, 2012.

Incidents involving deaths are further summarized in Table 7 by the location where the death occurred. The majority of non-fire, CO poisoning deaths (737 of 881, or 84%) reported to CPSC staff associated with engine-driven tools occurred at home locations. Seventy-one percent of the deaths occurred at fixed-structure residences, which includes single-family homes, apartments, townhouses, and mobile homes. Another 10 percent occurred in external structures at home locations, such as detached garages or sheds. And another two percent occurred in nontraditional homes, such as travel trailers, houseboats, or storage sheds used as permanent residences. The "Temporary shelter" category includes incidents in which victims died from CO poisoning from portable generators or other engine-driven tools while the victims were temporarily occupying trailers, horse trailers, recreational vehicles (RVs), cabins (used a temporary shelter), tents, and campers. Incidents that occurred in a temporary shelter, where the generator was an integral part of the temporary shelter, such as built-in generators or generators built specifically for use in an RV, were determined to be out of scope for this report and were excluded. The "Boat/Vehicle" category only includes incidents in which a generator or other engine-driven tool was not an integral part of the boat—but was brought onto the boat—and incidents where an EDT was brought into a vehicle, such as a van. As with temporary shelters, incidents involving generators that were built-in or specifically designed for a boat are not considered in scope and are not included in this report. The "Other" category includes incidents that occurred in the following locations: office buildings, utility buildings, and storage sheds (offsite from home).

Table 7: Number of Reported Non-Fire Carbon Monoxide Incidents and Fatalities Associated with Engine-Driven Tools by Location, 1999–*2011*

Location		Number of Incidents and Deaths Reported to CPSC							
		All Engine-Driven Tools		Generators		Other Engine-Driven Tools		Multiple Products[1,2]	
Total	Incidents	680	100%	513	100%	118	100%	49 (44)	100%
	Deaths	881	100%	695	100%	121	100%	65 (60)	100%
Home, fixed Structure[3]	Incidents	478	70%	372	73%	70	59%	36 (34)	73%
	Deaths	624	71%	506	73%	71	59%	47 (45)	72%
Home, detached Structure[4]	Incidents	87	13%	45	9%	38	32%	4 (1)	8%
	Deaths	91	10%	48	7%	39	32%	4 (1)	6%
Home, non-house[5]	Incidents	19	3%	13	3%	4	3%	2 (2)	4%
	Deaths	22	2%	16	2%	4	3%	2 (2)	3%
Temporary shelter	Incidents	61	9%	54	11%	2	2%	5 (5)	10%
	Deaths	95	11%	84	12%	2	2%	9 (9)	14%
Boat/Vehicle	Incidents	18	3%	15	3%	1	1%	2 (2)	4%
	Deaths	24	3%	19	3%	2	2%	3 (3)	5%
Other	Incidents	13	2%	11	2%	2	2%	0 (0)	0%
	Deaths	16	2%	14	2%	2	2%	0 (0)	0%
Not reported	Incidents	4	1%	3	1%	1	1%	0 (0)	0%
	Deaths	9	1%	8	1%	1	1%	0 (0)	0%

1   "Multiple Products" includes incidents involving generators or OEDTs with other CO-generating consumer products. "Other Consumer Products" includes one or more of the following: portable LP-fueled heaters, portable kerosene-fueled heaters, camp stoves, lanterns, outdoor cookers, furnaces, and wood stoves, and one case with a generator and another engine-driven tool (lawn mower) in operation.
2   Numbers in parentheses indicate incidents involving a generator and another product, including the case where a generator and an OEDT (lawn mower) were used concurrently.
3   This refers to a fixed-structure used as a residence, including: houses, mobile homes, apartments, townhouses, and structures attached to the house, such as an attached garage.
4   This refers to detached structures at home locations, including detached garages and sheds.
5   This refers to non-fixed location residences, including travel trailers and houseboats.
Notes: Totals may not add to 100 percent due to rounding.
    Italicized numbers indicate that reporting of incidents is ongoing. Counts may change in subsequent reports.
Source: U. S. Consumer Product Safety Commission, Directorate for Epidemiology, 2012.

Table 8 presents the number of non-fire, CO poisoning deaths reported to CPSC staff and associated with EDTs categorized by the population density of the place of death. All fatal incidents were assigned to one of four rural/urban categories, based on the Rural-Urban Commuting Area (RUCA) codes developed by the Economic Research Service (ERS) of the U.S. Department of Agriculture (USDA). Recently, the four urban/rural categories were changed to delineate further the large urban category. Formally, the four broad categories were "Urban," "Large Rural," "Small Rural," and "Isolated." In the newer categorization, the "Urban" category was divided into "Urban Core" and "Sub-Urban." Additionally, the "Small Rural" and "Isolated" categories are now combined into the "Small Rural/Isolated" category. Details on the process of determining population density, or rurality can be found at the USDA website at: http://www.ers.usda.gov/briefing/Rurality/. Additional information regarding the cross-referencing of zip codes to RUCA codes can be obtained from the University of Washington, WWAMI[4] Rural Health Research Center website at: http://depts.washington.edu/uwruca/.

Fifty-five percent (485 of 881) of CO fatalities associated with the use of engine-driven tools reported to CPSC staff occurred in urban areas while the estimated proportion of the U.S. population living in urban core areas is 71 percent. Forty-five percent (396 of 881) of CO fatalities occurred in non-urban core areas where an estimated 29 percent of the U.S. population lives. There appears to be an unusually high proportion of fatalities in small rural/isolated areas. Seventeen percent (149 of 881) of the CO fatalities known to CPSC staff to be associated with EDTs occurred in small rural and isolated areas where only an estimated nine percent of the U.S. population lives. The high proportion of fatalities in small rural/isolated areas can partly be explained by the fact that 23 percent of these occurred in temporary or boat/vehicle location and not in homes.

---

[4] The WWAMI name is derived from the first letter of each of the five cooperating states in a partnership between the University of Washington School of Medicine and the states of Wyoming, Alaska, Montana, and Idaho.

Table 8: Number of Reported Non-Fire Carbon Monoxide Fatalities Associated with Engine-Driven Tools by Population Density of Place of Death, 1999–*2011*

Population Density		Estimated Percentage of U.S. Population[1]	Number of Deaths Reported to CPSC							
			All Engine-Driven Tools		Generators		Other Engine-Driven Tools		Multiple Products[2,3]	
Total	Incident	100%	680	100%	513	100%	118	100%	49 (44)	100%
	Deaths		881	100%	695	100%	121	100%	65 (60)	100%
Urban Core	Incident	71%	369	54%	292	57%	59	50%	18 (18)	37%
	Deaths		485	55%	401	58%	60	50%	24 (24)	40%
Sub-Urban	Incident	10%	96	14%	68	13%	17	14%	11 (7)	22%
	Deaths		129	15%	97	14%	17	14%	15 (11)	24%
Large Rural	Incident	10%	99	15%	70	14%	19	16%	10 (9)	20%
	Deaths		118	13%	86	12%	20	17%	12 (11)	19%
Small Rural /Isolated	Incident	9%	116	17%	83	16%	23	19%	10 (10)	20%
	Deaths		149	17%	111	16%	24	20%	14 (14)	17%

1 Estimated 2010 U.S. population categorized by RUCA designation. U.S. population estimates by RUCA classification were determined from by cross-referencing the WWAMI RUCA zip code table with the 2010 U.S. Census population estimates by zip code area, the most current census data available by zip code area.

2 "Multiple Products" includes incidents involving generators or OEDTs with other CO-generating consumer products. "Other Consumer "Products" includes one or more of the following: portable LP-fueled heaters, portable kerosene-fueled heaters, camp stoves, lanterns, outdoor cookers, furnaces, and wood stoves, and one case with a generator and another engine-driven tool (lawn mower) in operation.

3 Numbers in parentheses indicate incidents involving a generator and another product, including the case where a generator and an OEDT (lawn mower) were being used concurrently.

Notes: Totals may not add to 100 percent due to rounding.

 Italicized numbers indicate that reporting of incidents is ongoing. Counts may change in subsequent reports.

Source: U. S. Consumer Product Safety Commission, Directorate for Epidemiology, 2012.

WWAMI Rural Research Center at the University of Washington Economic Research Group, USDA.

U.S. Census Bureau, 2011.

III. Alarm Usage

Table 9 presents a summary of CO fatalities known to CPSC staff characterized by CO alarm usage and alarm status. In 61 percent of the fatal incidents (415 of 680) and 58 percent of reported CO poisoning deaths (513 of 881), the presence of a CO alarm at the location of the incident was unknown or unreported. Of the 265 fatal incidents (368 CO fatalities) associated with engine-driven tools in which it was known whether a CO alarm was present or not, a CO alarm was present in only 21 incidents (8%) involving 30 CO fatalities. Of these 21 fatal incidents, the alarm was known to be inoperable in nine incidents (16 fatalities) due to missing or improperly installed batteries in a battery-powered alarm (non-plug-in type), or because the alarm was a plug-in type and power was out at the location of the incident. Seven of the nine fatal incidents (14 fatalities) with inoperable alarms were associated with generator usage.

For the remaining 12 fatal incidents (14 fatalities) where an alarm was known to be present, the alarm was known to have sounded in only six incidents (six deaths). Four of the six incidents occurred in an attached garage of a home with the alarm sounding inside the house. In one incident, the victim's family reportedly did not understand that the alarm sounding pattern (sounding every few minutes) was indicating CO present in the home and thought it simply meant that the alarm was working. In another incident, the victim was found in a home where a CO alarm was sounding. It is unclear if the alarm triggered after the victim became incapacitated by CO poisoning or if the victim simply misunderstood or ignored the signal. In an additional three CO deaths from three separate incidents, an apparently operable CO alarm failed to sound, even though lethal levels of CO were present in the home. There were also five deaths from three incidents in which a CO alarm was present in the house, but it was unknown whether it sounded or if it was even operable.

Table 9: Carbon Monoxide Alarm Usage Associated with Engine-Driven Tools Non-Fire Carbon Monoxide Poisoning Deaths, 1999–*2011*

CO Alarm Status	Number of Deaths and Percentage of Deaths when Alarm Status was Known											
	All Engine-Driven Tools			Generators			Other Engine-Driven Tools			Multiple Products[1,2]		
	Incidents	Deaths	% of Deaths	Incidents	Deaths	% of Deaths	Incidents	Deaths	% of Deaths	Incidents	Deaths	% of Deaths
Total	680	881	-	513	695	-	118	121	-	49 (44)	65 (60)	-
Alarm Status Known	265	368	100%	214	310	100%	31	33	100%	20 (17)	25 (22)	100%
No Alarm	244	338	92%	200	287	93%	28	30	91%	16 (14)	21 (19)	84%
Alarm Present	21	30	8%	14	23	7%	3	3	9%	4 (3)	4 (3)	16%
Alarmed	6	6	2%	2	2	1%	3	3	9%	1 (1)	1 (1)	4%
Did not alarm, batteries removed or incorrectly inserted	4	8	2%	3	7	2%	0	0	0%	1 (1)	1 (1)	4%
Did not alarm, plug-in type, no power	5	8	2%	4	7	2%	0	0	0%	1 (0)	1 (0)	4%
Did not alarm, though powered	3	3	1%	2	2	1%	0	0	0%	1 (1)	1 (1)	4%
Alarm present, Unknown if it alarmed	3	5	1%	3	5	2%	0	0	0%	0	0 (0)	0%
Alarm Status Unknown	415	513	-	299	385	-	87	88	-	29 (27)	40 (38)	-

1 "Multiple Products" includes incidents involving generators or OEDTs with other CO-generating consumer products. "Other Consumer Products" includes one or more of the following: portable LP-fueled heaters, portable kerosene-fueled heaters, camp stoves, lanterns, outdoor cookers, furnaces, and wood stoves, and one case with a generator and another engine-driven tool (lawn mower) in operation.

2 Numbers in parentheses indicate incidents involving a generator and another product, including the case where both a generator and an OEDT (lawn mower) were used concurrently.

Notes: Totals may not add to 100 percent due to rounding.

Italicized numbers indicate that reporting of incidents is ongoing. Counts may change in subsequent reports.

Source: U. S. Consumer Product Safety Commission, Directorate for Epidemiology, 2012.

IV. Hazard Patterns Associated with Generators

This section presents information about the usage patterns associated with fatal CO poisoning specific to generators, as well as information about the homes where fatal generator incidents occurred. As of April 20, 2012, CPSC staff is aware of 557 generator-related incidents in 1999 through 2011that resulted in non-fire CO fatalities. Five hundred-thirteen of these incidents involved only a generator. The remaining 44 incidents involved a generator and another combustion fuel-burning consumer product, including one that was another engine-driven tool. Staff completed In-depth Investigations (IDIs) for 520 of 557 (93%) fatal CO incidents associated with generators that occurred from 1999 through 2011. For the remaining 37 incidents in which an IDI was not performed or was not completed by the April 20, 2012 cut-off date, attempts were made to augment the data from reports of the incident in the Injury and Potential Injury Incidents (IPII) records or from death certificate information. Summaries of generator-related incidents in this section also include incidents where multiple fuel-burning consumer products were involved, including a generator.

A review of records for the 575 incidents resulting in 755 generator-related, non-fire CO deaths reported to CPSC staff, which includes 513 incidents (695 fatalities) involving a generator alone and 44 incidents (60 fatalities) involving a generator and another CO-producing consumer product, suggests two main reasons reported for using a generator. One reason cited was to provide electricity to a location that did not have electricity due to a temporary situation (*e.g.*, a power outage), and the other was to provide power after a shutoff to the residence by the utility company due to bill dispute or nonpayment. Table 10 provides a breakdown by year, listing the reasons why a generator was in use at the time of the incident. Twenty-nine percent (220 of the 755 reported deaths) of the generator-related, non-fire CO fatalities involved the use of generators during a temporary power outage stemming from a weather problem or a problem with power distribution. Nineteen percent (143 of 755 deaths) of the fatalities were associated with the use of generators after a power shutoff by the utility company for nonpayment. For 122 of the reported fatalities (16%), it could not be determined why the generator was in use, or why there was no electricity at the location of the incident.

Table 10: Number of Reported Non-Fire Carbon Monoxide Fatalities Associated with Generators[1] by Reason for Use, 1999–*2011*

Reason for Use		Total	1999	2000	2001	2002	2003	2004	2005	2006	2007	2008	2009	*2010*	*2011*
Total	Incidents	557	6	15	17	38	41	35	80	64	57	69	46	*35*	*54*
	Deaths	755	6	21	23	48	57	47	103	95	70	94	67	*44*	*80*
Power outage due to weather, or problem with power distribution	Incidents	154	3	1	3	12	15	7	37	11	15	19	10	*5*	*16*
	Deaths	220	3	1	3	16	20	11	53	17	23	26	17	*6*	*24*
Electricity turned off by power company due to bill dispute or nonpayment	Incidents	107	0	1	1	10	4	6	11	17	13	13	6	*11*	*14*
	Deaths	143	0	2	1	13	5	6	12	23	16	19	9	*15*	*22*
Provide power to storage shed, trailer, boat, camper, cabin, campsite	Incidents	78	0	7	6	5	8	3	8	14	8	5	8	*2*	*4*
	Deaths	113	0	11	9	7	10	4	11	21	9	7	11	*5*	*8*
New home or homeowner, and power not yet turned on, home under construction or renovation	Incidents	53	0	1	1	1	4	10	4	6	5	6	5	*5*	*5*
	Deaths	80	0	1	3	1	8	14	6	9	5	12	6	*5*	*10*
Provide power to home or mobile home that normally does not have electricity	Incidents	33	0	1	4	1	1	3	6	3	4	4	2	*3*	*1*
	Deaths	43	0	1	5	1	1	4	6	5	5	5	6	*3*	*1*
Working on or preparing a home for predicted storm	Incidents	7	1	0	0	0	1	0	0	1	0	4	0	*0*	*0*
	Deaths	7	1	0	0	0	1	0	0	1	0	4	0	*0*	*0*
Provide power to a shed or garage that normally does not have electricity	Incidents	8	0	1	1	1	0	0	0	0	0	2	0	*1*	*2*
	Deaths	8	0	1	1	1	0	0	0	0	0	2	0	*1*	*2*
Other (previous fire in house, power shut off by owners, servicing power supply, or other usage)	Incidents	16	1	2	1	3	0	0	1	1	0	3	2	*1*	*1*
	Deaths	19	1	3	1	4	0	0	1	1	0	3	2	*1*	*2*
Unknown why electricity off	Incidents	101	1	1	0	5	8	6	13	11	12	13	13	*7*	*11*
	Deaths	122	1	1	0	5	12	8	14	18	12	16	16	*8*	*11*

1   Number of deaths associated with generators includes incidents where other consumer products may also have been involved. Other products include one or more of the following: lawn mowers, portable LP-fueled heaters, portable kerosene-fueled heaters, camp stoves, lanterns, outdoor cookers, furnaces, and wood stoves.
Notes: Totals may not add to 100 percent due to rounding.
       Italicized numbers indicate that reporting of incidents is ongoing. Counts may change in subsequent reports.
Source: U. S. Consumer Product Safety Commission, Directorate for Epidemiology, 2012.

For the 220 fatalities associated with a power outage due to weather or a problem with power distribution, Table 11 provides a further breakdown by year and cause of the power outage. Ninety-one percent (201 of 220) of the fatalities associated with power outages were due to specific weather conditions. Ice or snow storms are associated with the largest percentage of weather-related CO fatalities (47%). From 2006 to 2011, the percentage of weather-related CO fatalities associated with ice and snow storms is even higher at 54percent (61 of 113). Hurricanes are also associated with a large percentage of CO fatalities (29%) over the 13-year period from 1999 to 2011. But nearly half of the hurricane- or tropical storm-related fatalities (31 of 63) occurred in 2005.

Table 11: Number of Reported Non-Fire Carbon Monoxide Fatalities Associated with Generators[1] by Reason for Power Outage, 1999–*2011*

Reason for Power Outage		Total	1999	2000	2001	2002	2003	2004	2005	2006	2007	2008	2009	*2010*	*2011*
Total	Incidents	154	3	1	3	12	15	7	37	11	15	19	10	*5*	*16*
	Deaths	220	3	1	3	16	20	11	53	17	23	26	17	*6*	*24*
Ice or snow storm	Incidents	74	0	0	0	10	5	1	15	6	9	7	9	*3*	*9*
	Deaths	104	0	0	0	14	7	2	20	8	13	9	14	*4*	*13*
Hurricane or tropical storm	Incidents	42	0	0	0	1	6	5	20	1	0	6	0	*0*	*3*
	Deaths	63	0	0	0	1	9	8	31	1	0	8	0	*0*	*5*
Wind storm	Incidents	6	0	0	1	0	0	0	0	2	1	1	0	*0*	*1*
	Deaths	10	0	0	1	0	0	0	0	6	1	1	0	*0*	*1*
Thunderstorm or rainstorm	Incidents	11	0	0	1	0	2	0	1	2	1	1	0	*2*	*1*
	Deaths	13	0	0	1	0	2	0	1	2	1	2	0	*2*	*2*
Tornado	Incidents	3	0	0	0	0	0	0	0	0	0	2	0	*0*	*1*
	Deaths	5	0	0	0	0	0	0	0	0	0	3	0	*0*	*2*
Storm, unspecified	Incidents	4	0	0	0	0	0	0	0	0	2	1	0	*0*	*1*
	Deaths	6	0	0	0	0	0	0	0	0	4	1	0	*0*	*1*
Unknown or other reason for outage	Incidents	14	3	1	1	1	2	1	1	0	2	1	1	*0*	*0*
	Deaths	19	3	1	1	1	2	1	1	0	4	2	3	*0*	*0*

1   Number of deaths associated with generators includes incidents where other consumer products may also have been involved. Other products include one or more of the following: lawn mowers, portable LP-fueled heaters, portable kerosene-fueled heaters, camp stoves, lanterns, outdoor cookers, furnaces, and wood stoves.

Note: Italicized numbers indicate that reporting of incidents is ongoing. Counts may change in subsequent reports.

Source: U.S. Consumer Product Safety Commission, Directorate for Epidemiology, 2012.

In 2005, the number of power outage-related fatalities jumped to 53, with 52 known to be weather related. The 52 fatalities associated with weather-related power outages in 2005 were due primarily to hurricanes in September in the Gulf states, ice/snow storms in January in the Midwest, and ice storms in December in the Carolinas. Figure 2 illustrates the impact of the power outages in 2005, relative to other years. The 31 hurricane- or tropical storm-related, non-fire CO fatalities in 2005 that CPSC staff is aware of constitute more CO deaths than for any other year in this report for all weather-related outages combined. An additional 20 fatalities were associated with the use of generators during ice- or snow-related power outages in 2005, the highest total for any year covered in this report.

Figure 2: Number of Reported Non-Fire Carbon Monoxide Fatalities Associated with Generators Usage During Power Outages

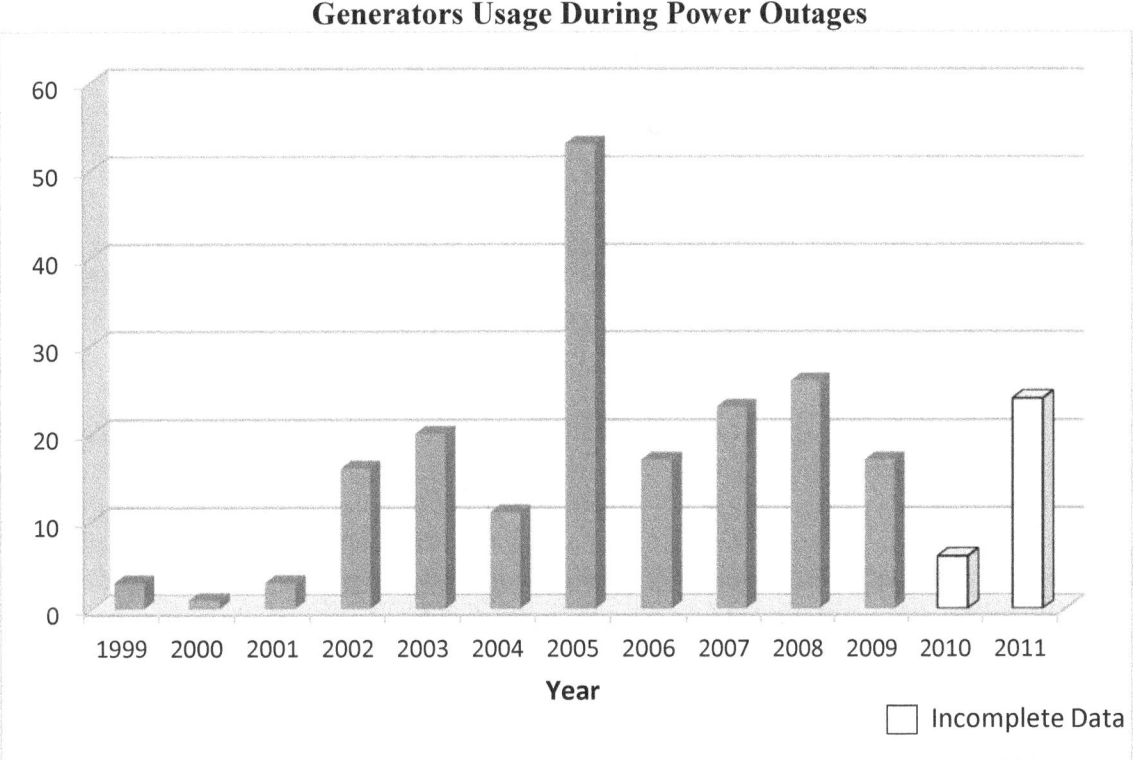

Table 7 shows 506 generator-related, non-fire CO fatalities that occurred in a fixed-structure home. For this characterization, a "fixed-structure home" is defined as a permanent, fixed residential structure, including detached and attached houses, apartments, fixed mobile homes, and cabins used as a permanent residence. Travel trailers, campers, and RVs are not included in this classification. Additionally, 45 of the 47 multiple product-related fatalities involved a generator in a fixed-structure home. Of these 551 generator-related fatalities (406 incidents) that occurred in a fixed-structure home, information was available for 469 deaths (85%, from 342 incidents) regarding the victim's location in relation to the generator. One hundred-eight of these 469 fatalities (23%) occurred in the same room or space as the generator.

The 551 deaths that occurred in a fixed-structure home were further classified by the specific location of the generator (Table 12) within the home. The category "Living Space" includes rooms reported as bedrooms, bathrooms, dens, living rooms, landings, home offices, rear rooms, enclosed porches, and converted garages. This category does not include attached garages or basements. The category "Outside Home" includes incidents where the generator was placed outside a home but near an open window, door, or vent of the home. Seventy percent (385 of 551) of the CO deaths at home locations occurred when a generator was placed inside the home, including the living space (173), a basement (153), closet (13), doorway (6), or inside the house, with no further information provided (40). Another 24 percent (131 of 551) occurred when the generator was placed in an attached garage, enclosed carport, or attached barn. More than half of the CO fatalities (284 of 551) occurred when the generator was placed in an attached structure (131), or in the basement or crawlspace (153).

Review of the yearly fatal incident data in Table 12 suggests that since 2004, more fatalities were related to generators in living areas of the home. Included in the definition of "non-basement living area of the home" are the categories "Living Space," "Closet of Home," and "Doorway of Home." Not included is the category "Inside house, no further information reported" because this could be in the living area or the basement of the house. From 2000 through 2003, there were more CO fatalities reported where the generator was placed in the basement or crawl space than in the non-basement living areas (in 1999, there were an equal number of fatalities reported where generators were placed in the basement and the living area). For each of the years 2004 through 2011, more reported CO fatalities were associated with generators in non-basement living areas than in basement or crawl space locations. Of the 109 generator-associated fatalities between 1999 and 2003, the basement was the predominant location of the generator (48 of 109, or 44%), followed by living areas (23 of 109, or 21%), including living space (17), closets (2), and doorways (4), and attached garages and other attached structures (22 of 109, or 20%). Thirteen deaths were associated with the use of a generator placed outside of the home. Usually, this involved placing the generator too near an open window or vent. This category also includes incidents where a generator was running outside the home but inside a building (*e.g.*, outside an apartment but still inside the building). From 2004 onward, there have been 442 reported CO fatalities in the home associated with the use of generators. More CO fatalities occurred with the generators placed in the non-basement living areas (169 of 442, or 38%, including living space (156), closets (11), and doorways (2)), followed by an attached garage or other structure (109 of 442, or 25%), and then the basement (105 of 442, or 24%). It is unclear why there has been a shift from the basement to the living space, but this may indicate a lack of knowledge by consumers about the severity of the CO dangers associated with the use of generators inside the home.

Table 12: Non-Fire Carbon Monoxide Poisoning Deaths in the Fixed-structure Home Location[1] by Location of the Generator,[2] 1999–*2011*

Generator Location		Total	1999	2000	2001	2002	2003	2004	2005	2006	2007	2008	2009	*2010*	*2011*
Total	Incidents	406	5	5	8	32	32	28	55	40	43	51	36	*28*	*43*
	Deaths	551	5	7	10	41	46	38	70	57	55	70	53	*34*	*65*
Living space (non-basement)	Incidents	131	2	1	2	5	6	12	17	12	15	20	13	*13*	*13*
	Deaths	173	2	1	2	5	7	18	23	17	19	27	19	*13*	*20*
Garage / enclosed carport / attached barn	Incidents	100	0	1	2	8	7	6	17	13	9	13	8	*4*	*12*
	Deaths	130	0	2	2	10	8	8	18	20	14	15	11	*5*	*17*
Basement / crawlspace	Incidents	101	2	3	2	12	12	6	12	9	9	11	6	*4*	*13*
	Deaths	153	2	4	4	18	20	7	15	11	12	20	11	*7*	*22*
Inside house, no further information reported	Incidents	33	1	0	1	3	5	1	2	4	6	4	3	*1*	*2*
	Deaths	39	1	0	1	4	7	1	2	4	6	4	5	*2*	*2*
Closet in home	Incidents	6	0	0	0	2	0	0	1	1	1	0	1	*0*	*0*
	Deaths	13	0	0	0	2	0	0	6	3	1	0	1	*0*	*0*
Outdoors	Incidents	11	0	0	1	0	1	1	4	0	2	0	0	*1*	*1*
	Deaths	14	0	0	1	0	2	2	4	0	2	0	0	*1*	*2*
Doorway to home	Incidents	5	0	0	0	2	1	1	0	1	0	0	0	*0*	*0*
	Deaths	7	0	0	0	2	2	1	0	2	0	0	0	*0*	*0*
Unknown location, but at home	Incidents	19	0	0	0	0	0	1	2	0	1	3	5	*5*	*2*
	Deaths	22	0	0	0	0	0	1	2	0	1	4	6	*6*	*2*

1 This refers to a fixed-structure used as a residence, including houses, mobile homes, apartments, townhouses, and structures attached to the house, such as an attached garage. Not included here are incidents that occurred in detached structures at home locations (*e.g.,* detached garages, sheds) or at non-fixed location residences (*e.g.,* travel trailers, houseboats).

2 Number of deaths associated with generators includes incidents where other consumer products may also have been involved. Other products include one or more of the following: lawn mowers, portable LP-fueled heaters, portable kerosene-fueled heaters, camp stoves, lanterns, outdoor cookers, furnaces, and wood stoves.

Notes: Totals may not add to 100 percent due to rounding.

Italicized numbers indicate that reporting of incidents is ongoing. Counts may change in subsequent reports.

Source: U. S. Consumer Product Safety Commission, Directorate for Epidemiology, 2012.

Table 13 presents a summary of non-fire CO fatalities that occurred in the fixed-structure home characterized by ventilation status. Many of the incidents of generator-associated fatalities in the home (239 of the 551 deaths) did not contain information about the ventilation of the generator. In 205 of the 312 deaths (66%) in which information on ventilation of the generator was available, the generators were not vented at the time of the incident. In four of these deaths, a window or door was open during some period of use but later closed. There were 107 deaths associated with generators in which it was reported that some type of ventilation was employed. Of these 107 deaths, 82 non-fire CO deaths were associated with incidents in which it was reported that there was an open or partially open window, door, garage door, or a combination of these. Fourteen deaths were associated with generators that were placed outside the home near open windows, doors, or vents, where carbon monoxide entered the home. In 17 deaths (from 7 incidents), consumers actively attempted to vent generator exhaust outside through a window or door, or through the use of a fan, but these measures failed to adequately vent the CO from the victims' location. An additional fatality occurred when a victim placed a generator outside of an apartment in the unventilated hallway of a building.

Table 13: Non-Fire CO Fatalities in the Fixed-structure Home[1] Reported to CPSC Staff and Associated with Generators[2] Categorized by Status of Ventilation, 1999–*2011*

Ventilation Status	Number of Incidents	Number of Deaths	Percentage of Deaths	Percentage of Deaths Where Ventilation is Known
Non-fire CO fatalities in the home	**406**	**551**	**100%**	**100%**
Some ventilation attempted	**73**	**101**	**18%**	**32%**
Open window(s), open door(s), an open garage door, or a combination of these	54	69	13%	22%
Actively trying to vent either by fans or by directing exhaust out a window or door	7	17	3%	5%
Placed outside, but near a window, door or A/C unit[3]	11	14	3%	4%
Placed outside apartment, but inside building	1	1	< 1%	< 1%
No ventilation	**157**	**215**	**39%**	**68%**
Open windows or doors closed sometime later	5	7	1%	2%
No ventilation attempted[4]	152	208	38%	66%
Unknown ventilation	**176**	**235**	**43%**	**-**

1   This refers to a fixed-location structure used as a residence, including houses, mobile homes, apartments, and townhouses, as well as structures attached to the house, such as an attached garage. Not included here are incidents that occurred in detached structures at home locations (*e.g.,* detached garages and sheds) or at non-fixed location residences (*e.g.,* travel trailers and houseboats).
2   Number of deaths associated with generators includes incidents where other consumer products may also have been involved. Other products include one or more of the following: lawn mowers, portable LP fueled heaters, portable kerosene fueled heaters, camp stoves, lanterns, outdoor cookers, furnaces, and wood stoves.
3   One incident involved alternately moving the generator outside then inside after the generator would shut off, presumably because of weather conditions. After a warm-up period, the generator was again placed outside until it failed again.
4   One death occurred when a generator was placed outside an apartment in an unvented hallway and one occurred when the generator was placed outside a trailer that was located inside an enclosed, unvented garage.
Source: U. S. Consumer Product Safety Commission, Directorate for Epidemiology, 2012.
Note: Italicized numbers indicate that reporting of incidents is ongoing. Counts may change in subsequent reports.

Table 14 presents a summary of the fatal CO incidents and fatalities characterized by the size of the home in which the fatalities occurred. For 36 percent (198 of 551) of the deaths (149 of 406 fatal incidents), CPSC staff could not ascertain the size of the home. Home size information was available for 353 of the 551 deaths (257 of 406 fatal incidents). Information regarding the size of the home reported in this document is from one of two sources. The first source is the CPSC In-depth Investigations (IDIs), which include information gathered from police, fire department, or public records. The second source is from Internet databases of real estate information, which contain public record data, such as *Cyberhomes.com* and *Zillow.com*. In most cases, Internet databases agree on the size of the home because both databases are based on public records from the county, state, or municipality. Occasionally, the records in the databases do not agree. In that situation, the average of the two or more sizes was used because it could not be determined which database had the more accurate figure.

Sixty-one percent (215 of 353) of the reported CO fatalities (from 154 of the 257 fatal incidents) associated with generators that occurred in the home, where the size of the structure was known, occurred in homes that were less than 1,500 square feet, and 84 percent (298 of 353 deaths from 219 of the 257 incidents) occurred in houses that were less than 2,000 square feet. This portion of the fatal incident location includes most incidents that occurred in apartments and mobile homes. Fatal incidents that occurred in a detached structure are not included in this figure. The median home size involved in fatal CO poisoning deaths, where home size information is known, was 1,350 square feet. As a point of reference, according to the U.S. Census Bureau's *American Housing Survey for the United States: 2009*, the median housing unit as of 2009 was 1,736 square feet. Comparing the percentages of fatal incidents by home size to the U.S. Census figures, it appears that the fatal CO incidents are skewed toward smaller homes. Whether this is due to economic reasons or because smaller-volume structures are more quickly filled by deadly carbon monoxide, is unclear. Perhaps it is a combination of the two factors, or some yet unidentified reason.

Table 14: Non-Fire CO Fatalities in the Fixed-structure Home[1] Reported to CPSC Staff and Associated with Generators[2] Categorized by Size of Home, 1999–*2011*

Home Size (in sq. feet)[2]	Number of Incidents	Number of Deaths	Percentage of Incidents	Percentage of Incidents Where Home Size is Known	Estimated Percentage of U.S. Housing Units (2009)[4]
Total	406	551	100%	100%	100%
Under 500	1	1	< 1%	< 1%	1%
500–999	57	73	14%	22%	10%
1,000–1,499	96	141	24%	37%	25%
1,500–1,999	65	83	16%	25%	24%
2,000–2,499	26	41	6%	10%	17%
2,500–2,999	5	6	1%	2%	9%
3,000 or Larger	7	8	2%	3%	14%
Unknown	149	198	37%	-	-

1   This refers to a fixed-location structure used as a residence, including houses, mobile homes, apartments, and townhouses and structures attached to the house, such as an attached garage. Not included here are incidents that occurred in detached structures at home locations (*e.g.*, detached garages and sheds) or at non-fixed location residences (*e.g.*, travel trailers and houseboats).
2   Number of deaths associated with generators includes incidents where other consumer products may also have been involved. Other products include one or more of the following: lawn mowers, portable LP-fueled heaters, portable kerosene-fueled heaters, camp stoves, lanterns, outdoor cookers, furnaces, and wood stoves.
3   Home size based on CPSC IDIs or from the Internet real estate databases, *Cyberhomes.com* and *Zillow.com.*
4   The 2009 housing unit figures are the most current figures available.
Source: U. S. Consumer Product Safety Commission, Directorate for Epidemiology, 2012.
        U.S. Census Bureau, American Housing Survey for the United States: 2009.
Note: Italicized numbers indicate that reporting of incidents is ongoing. Counts may change in subsequent reports.

The size of the generator and the fuel used with the generator were both examined. The size of the generator was examined by the wattage rating (Table 15). In most cases, the advertised running wattage rating was used to categorize the generator. In some instances, however, a wattage rating was used in which it could not be determined whether it was the rated running wattage or maximum/surge wattage. When the wattage rating of the generator was known or could be determined (367 investigated deaths from 252 incidents), two-thirds of the deaths (245, 168 incidents) were associated with a generator in the 3500 to 6499 watt rating range. Nearly half (168 or 46%, 117 incidents) of the CO fatalities, where the generator size was known, were associated with generators in the 5000 to 6499 watt range. Generator sales data available to CPSC staff[5] indicate that during the time period 2003 through 2005, 56 percent of portable generators sold to consumers were in the 3500 to 6499 watt range; 23 percent of units sold had outputs below 3500 watts; and 21 percent had outputs of 6500 watts or greater. During this same period, generator size is available for incidents associated with 92 fatalities from 66 incidents. Seventy-eight percent (72 of 92, 49 incidents) of the CO fatalities were associated with generators in the 3500 to 6499 watt range; 20 percent (18 of 92, 15 incidents) were associated with units with outputs below 3500 watts; and 2 percent (2 of 92, 2 incidents) were associated with units with outputs of 6500 watts or greater. In the time period following the sales data (2006 through 2011), there were 216 fatalities from 143 incidents in which the generator size is known. Of these, 63 percent (135 of 216, 93 incidents) of

---

5 Smith, Charles L. *Portable Electric Generator Sets for Consumer Use: Additional Data on Annual Sales, Number in Use, and Societal Costs.* Memorandum to Janet Buyer, Project Manager, ESFS. August 24, 2006.

CO fatalities were associated with generators in the 3500 to 6499 watt range; 28 percent (61 of 216, 38 incidents) were associated with units with outputs below 3500 watts; and 9 percent (20 of 216, 12 incidents) were associated with units with outputs of 6500 watts or greater. Assessments of trends or patterns using direct comparisons of sales data and CO fatality data should be made with caution. Sales figures only reflect the proportion of newly purchased generators in each category and do not reflect the proportions of existing generators in the consumer population. Although many CO fatalities are associated with first-time users of newly purchased generators, many are also associated with older generators originally purchased for other uses or borrowed when a need for power presented itself.

Almost all of the generators that were involved in the CO poisoning incidents identified in this report were referred to as gas- or gasoline-fueled generators. One generator was identified as a propane-fueled generator, and one was identified as a natural gas-fueled generator.

Table 15: Number of Reported Non-Fire Carbon Monoxide Fatalities Associated with Generators[1] Categorized by Generator Wattage Rating, 1999–2011

Wattage Rating (in Watts)		Total	1999	2000	2001	2002	2003	2004	2005	2006	2007	2008	2009	2010	2011
Total	Incidents	557	6	15	17	38	41	35	80	64	57	69	46	35	54
	Deaths	755	6	21	23	48	57	47	103	95	70	94	67	44	80
Under 2000	Incidents	18	0	2	0	3	0	2	3	1	2	1	1	2	1
	Deaths	21	0	2	0	3	0	2	3	1	5	1	1	2	1
2000–3499	Incidents	51	0	3	3	5	2	2	6	9	5	5	3	2	6
	Deaths	78	0	5	3	7	3	2	8	17	6	8	6	2	11
3500–4999	Incidents	51	0	1	4	1	3	2	10	6	4	9	2	3	6
	Deaths	77	0	2	8	1	5	2	13	11	7	11	2	5	10
5000–6499	Incidents	117	1	3	3	13	11	11	12	15	9	13	8	9	9
	Deaths	168	1	3	4	19	14	18	20	20	9	19	15	11	15
6500–7999	Incidents	9	0	0	0	0	0	0	1	0	1	3	1	1	2
	Deaths	13	0	0	0	0	0	0	1	0	2	4	1	1	4
8000 and larger	Incidents	6	0	0	0	1	0	1	0	1	0	1	1	0	1
	Deaths	10	0	0	0	1	0	1	0	1	0	1	1	0	5
Not reported	Incidents	305	5	6	7	15	25	17	48	32	36	37	30	18	29
	Deaths	388	5	9	8	17	35	22	58	45	41	50	41	23	34

1   Number of deaths associated with generators includes incidents where other consumer products may also have been involved. Other products include one or more of the following: lawn mowers, portable LP-fueled heaters, portable kerosene-fueled heaters, camp stoves, lanterns, outdoor cookers, furnaces, and wood stoves.
Source: U. S. Consumer Product Safety Commission, Directorate for Epidemiology, 2012.
Note: Italicized numbers indicate that reporting of incidents is ongoing. Counts may change in subsequent reports.

Conclusion

Between 1999 and 2011, there were 881 non-fire CO poisoning deaths reported to CPSC staff that were associated with engine-driven tools. The majority of these deaths (695) involved generators. Another 60 fatalities were associated with both a generator and another consumer product (one involved both a generator and another engine-driven tool). Other engine-driven tools, including garden tractors, lawn mowers, power washers or sprayers, and others, were associated with a much smaller number of deaths. The majority of fatal incidents reported to CPSC staff involved a single fatality. Most reported deaths occurred while an individual was at home.

Victims age 25 years and older accounted for about 82 percent of the non-fire CO poisoning deaths that were associated with generators reported to CPSC staff, and the majority (73%) of the victims were male. Seventy-three percent of the reported deaths associated with generators (including deaths associated with the use of a generator and another consumer product) occurred at fixed-structure home locations. Seventy percent of the fatalities known to have occurred in the home involving generators occurred when a generator was placed in the living area or basement of the home. Another 24 percent occurred when a generator was used inside an attached garage or shed.

Generators were often used as alternative sources of electricity due to temporary power outages or as power sources for temporary shelters. Power outages, most commonly weather-related, were the single most common reason for generator usage that resulted in a non-fire CO fatality, accounting for at least 220 of the 755 fatalities (29%). Generators were often used with little or no ventilation. In only about 7 percent of the fatalities was it known that there was a CO alarm installed—and most of these were inoperable at the time of the fatal incident. Conclusions about why consumers used generators indoors or determinations about whether users were aware of the potential non-fire CO-poisoning hazard are difficult to make with the available information.

Victims age 25 years and older accounted for 99 percent (120 of 121) of the non-fire CO poisoning deaths reported to CPSC staff that were associated with other engine-driven tools. Males accounted for 97 percent (117 of 121) of the deaths associated with other engine-driven tools. Deaths associated with garden tractors and lawn mowers were often associated with an individual repairing or working on the product in an enclosed space.

Visit the CPSC's Carbon Monoxide Information Center—www.cpsc.gov/info/co/index.html—for the latest information on recalls, safety tips, safety standards, CO alarms, and downloadable injury prevention materials.

References

Hnatov, Matthew V. *Incidents, Deaths, and In-Depth Investigations Associated with Non-Fire Carbon Monoxide from Engine-Driven Generators and Other Engine-Driven Tools, 1999-2010.* U.S. Consumer Product Safety Commission. July 2011.

Hnatov, Matthew V. *Non-Fire Carbon Monoxide Deaths Associated with the Use of Consumer Products: 2008 Annual Estimates.* U.S. Consumer Product Safety Commission. January 2012.

Smith, Charles L. *Portable Electric Generator Sets for Consumer Use: Additional Data on Annual Sales, Number in Use, and Societal Costs.* Memorandum to Janet Buyer, Project Manager, Directorate for Engineering Sciences, Division of Combustion and Fire Sciences. August 24, 2006.

U.S. Census Bureau. American FactFinder. Population, Housing Units, Area, and Density: 2010 - State -- 5-digit ZIP Code Tabulation Area: 2010 Census Summary File 1
<http://factfinder2.census.gov/faces/tableservices/jsf/pages/productview.xhtml?pid=DEC_10_SF1_GCTPH1.ST09&prodType=table>

U.S. Census Bureau. American Housing Survey for the United States: 2009.
<http://www.census.gov/prod/2011pubs/h150-09.pdf>

U.S. Department of Agriculture. Briefing Rooms: Measuring Rurality. 7 Nov. 2008
<http://www.ers.usda.gov/briefing/Rurality/>

University of Washington, WWAMI Rural Health Research Center. Guidelines for Using Rural-Urban Classification Systems for Public Health Assessment 15 Feb. 2011
<http://www.doh.wa.gov/data/guidelines/RuralUrban2.htm>

Goodman, David C., *2008 Population Estimates for Zip Code Tabulation Areas (ZCTAs) and Primary Care Service Areas (PCSAs).* Health Resources and Services Administration. 1 May 2009

Appendix A: Epidemiology Data Retrieval Specifics

The queries below were submitted through EPIR (EPIdemiology Retrieval), the CPSC staff's epidemiology data access application. Query results were reviewed to include only carbon monoxide poisoning incidents and to exclude duplicates and out-of-scope cases, which were cases that did not involve an incident that was associated with a non-fire carbon monoxide exposure and an engine-driven tool. Records from the three databases that were used in this report (the In-depth Investigation database (INDP), the Injury or Potential Injury Incident database (IPII), and the Death Certificate database (DTHS)) were then manually matched up to provide the most complete record and to eliminate additional duplicates.

For this report, a fatal incident was deemed in scope if none of the following criteria were violated:
- Carbon monoxide was the primary or contributing factor in the fatality,
- The carbon monoxide was not fire-related,
- The source of the CO was an engine-driven tool, or an engine-driven tool used in conjunction with another non-fire-related CO generating source,
- The fatal injury was unintentional in nature,
- The engine-driven tool involved was a consumer product, and
- The incident was not work-related.

Date of Queries: 04/20/2012

Incident Dates: 1/1/99-12/31/11
Product Codes: 113, 606, 800-899, 1062, 1400-1464, 3285-3287
Diagnosis Codes: 65 (Anoxia), 68 (Poisoning) – (INDP only)
ICD10 Code: X47x, Y17x – (DTHS only)
Narrative/Text Contains: 'CARB' or 'MONO'

Appendix B: Carboxyhemoglobin Levels Present In CO Fatalities

Carboxyhemoglobin (COHb) is a complex of carbon monoxide and hemoglobin that forms in red blood cells when carbon monoxide is inhaled. COHb poisoning can be fatal in large doses as it hinders delivery of oxygen to the body. Carboxyhemoglobin data is helpful in estimating the concentration of CO in the product exhaust and the lethality of the product which affects the speed of onset of harm. This information may be used by CPSC staff to assist in determining how best to address the CO hazard presented by generators and other engine-driven tools.

In healthy adults, a COHb level of 40–50 percent in the blood approximately correlates with symptoms of confusion, unconsciousness, coma, and possible death; a level of 50–70 percent approximately correlates with symptoms of coma, brain damage, seizure, and death; and a level greater than 70 percent is typically fatal.[6] COHb levels were available for 499 of the 881 fatalities (57% of the CO fatalities). Table B-1 shows the frequency of reports by COHb level categories. Percentages in the table are the category proportions of reported COHb levels. Eighty-one percent (405 of the 499) of fatalities had reported COHb levels of 50 percent or greater.

---

[6] Inkster S.E. *Health hazard assessment of CO poisoning associated with emissions from a portable, 5.5 Kilowatt, gasoline-powered generator.* Washington, D.C.: U.S. Consumer Product Safety Commission. 2004.

Table B-1: Carboxyhemoglobin Levels Associated with Engine-Driven Tools Non-Fire Carbon Monoxide Poisoning Deaths, 1999–*2011*

COHb Level	Number of Deaths[1]							
	All Engine-Driven Tools		Generators		Other Engine-Driven Tools		Multiple Products[2,3]	
Total	881	-	695	-	121	-	65 (60)	-
Reported Levels	499	100%	391	100%	69	100%	39 (34)	100%
Less than 30%	23	5%	18	5%	2	3%	3 (3)	8%
30–39.9%	28	6%	23	6%	4	6%	1 (1)	3%
40–49.9%	43	9%	34	9%	9	13%	0 (0)	0%
50–59.9%	100	20%	81	21%	11	16%	8 (8)	21%
60–69.9%	137	27%	110	28%	16	23%	11 (8)	28%
70–79.9%	130	26%	97	25%	18	26%	15 (13)	38%
80–89.9%	34	7%	24	6%	9	13%	1 (1)	3%
90–99.9%	4	1%	4	1%	0	0%	0 (0)	0%
Not reported	382	-	304	-	52	-	26 (26)	-

1 Percentages shown are the percentage of reported COHb levels per category.
2 "Multiple Products" includes incidents involving generators or OEDTs with other CO generating consumer products. Other consumer products include one or more of the following: portable LP fueled heaters, portable kerosene fueled heaters, camp stoves, lanterns, outdoor cookers, furnaces, and wood stoves, and one case with both a generator and another engine-driven tool (lawn mower) in operation.
3 Numbers in parentheses indicate incidents involving a generator and another product, including the case where a generator and an OEDT (lawn mower) were used concurrently.
Notes: Totals may not add to 100 percent due to rounding.
     Italicized numbers indicate that reporting of incidents is ongoing. Counts may change in subsequent reports.
Source: U. S. Consumer Product Safety Commission, Directorate for Epidemiology, 2012.

www.ingramcontent.com/pod-product-compliance
Lightning Source LLC
Chambersburg PA
CBHW081804280526
45789CB00008B/2987